MORTGAGE MUMBO-JUMBO

Expert Strategies to Find The Best Mortgage

JAKE TAYLOR

Jacobs & Whitehall
73-03 Bell Blvd, #10
Oakland Gardens, NY 11364
www.jacobsandwhitehall.com

Ordering Information:
Quantity sales. Special discounts are available on quantity purchases by corporations, associations, and others. For details, contact the publisher at the address above.

Orders by U.S. trade bookstores and wholesalers. Please contact Jacobs & Whitehall: Tel: (888) 991-2766 or visit www.jacobsandwhitehall.com.

Printed in the United States of America

Published in 2020

ISBN: 978-1-951149-55-0

Dedication

Although it may seem hopeless at first, or the beginning of a never-ending road, you CAN pay off your mortgage, even a few years sooner than you think, without a tremendous effort.

Once you pay off your mortgage and discover how to save yourself years of time and tens of thousands of interest payments, you're going to feel the wind of financial freedom pushing you forward towards a prosperous future.

This book is dedicated to the American Dream, and the dream of owning your home free and clear.

DISCLAIMER

This publication is intended to be used for educational purposes only. No legal advice is being given, and no attorney-client relationship is intended to be created by reading this material. The author assumes no liability for any errors or omissions or for how this book or its contents are used or interpreted, or for any consequences resulting directly or indirectly from the use of this book. For legal or any other advice, please consult an experienced attorney or the appropriate expert, who is aware of the specific facts of your case and is knowledgeable in the law in your jurisdiction.

Pilot Mortgage, LLC
727 W Ray Rd #B7
Gilbert, AZ
(480) 999-3339
www.jaketaylor.com

TESTIMONIALS

"Jake Taylor and his team at Pilot Mortgage are hands down the best! I have bought 7 houses and used big banks, and other mortgage brokers and they were ok at best. Jake's customer service is on a whole different level. He takes time to explain the best options and ways to save money. I once received a call out of the blue from Jake and he explained how he could refinance my house and save me thousands of dollars. I have referred my Mom, dad, brother, and many close friends to Jake over the years and will continue to do so. I don't even bother calling other companies anymore because I know Jake will get me the best rates possible. Thank you, Jake, for always looking out for me and my family."

– *Adam Miller*

****

"Jake has been doing mortgages for the past 18 consecutive years, and what I have heard over and over from our friends who are repeat clients of his is that he knows the business better than anyone else. If there is a better program, more money to be saved, or a better rate available, Jake will know about it. His transactions close quickly and smoothly, and I have seen and heard him turn the most novice, anxious buyers into trusting and loyal clients who refer their own friends and family members. He earns everyone's trust because he is honest and knowledgeable and there is simply no substitute for good character and decades of experience."

– *Elisa Starr Taylor*

****

"Jake helped us improve our credit rating in a very short period of time to qualify for a better loan percentage rate. He reviewed all of our debt and created a plan for us to pay down certain debt in order to raise our FICO score. By just paying down a couple of debts to lower our debt ratio, our FICO score improved significantly. We are on our way to buying a new home."

– Daniel Magallanes

****

"I highly recommend Jake he made my refinancing so easy and fast in less than 30 days I'm now waiting for my close date. He always answered my texts and questions right away which was super important to me to receive answers timely since customer service is so important to me. Very happy customer!!"

– Debbie Ashton

****

Table Of Contents

i.	**Dedication**	**3**
ii.	**Disclaimer**	**4**
iii.	**Testimonials**	**5**
iv.	**Table Of Contents**	**7**
v.	**About The Author**	**9**
1.	**What Are Major Types Of Loans?**	**11**
2.	**When Do Jumbo Loans Come Into Play?**	**16**
3.	**What Are Conventional Or Conforming Loans?**	**19**
4.	**When Is Mortgage Insurance Required?**	**23**
5.	**What Are FHA Loans For?**	**26**
6.	**What's A USDA Loan?**	**30**
7.	**What's A VA Loan And Who Qualifies?**	**34**

8. **What Are The Consequences Of Refinancing?** 39

vi. **Index** 46

vii. **Notes** 48

About The Author

I make my home in Arizona with four beautiful children and my wife. A graduate of ASU, I'm also a US Army Veteran. I've been a mortgage broker since 2001 and have handled close to 1,500 loans for my clients. The average amount I handle is approximately $12 million per year; therfore, throughout my career I have helped borrowers gain access to over $200 million in loans thus far.

At Pilot Mortgage, we handle a wide range of loans for our clients. These include reverse mortgages for seniors, FHA loans, USDA loans for those buying in rural areas, and VA loans. We also meet the needs of those seeking conventional loans as well as those looking for loans that are larger than the average amount. Pilot Mortgage also performs loan services for self-employed individuals as well as bank statement loans, or stated income loans, for people buying investment properties. Lastly, we also handle commercial loans, though this is not the core of our business. We do everything, really. If there's a property with a commercial use or a residential use, we will work towards an effective loan for that property.

Chapter 1

What Are Major Types Of Loans?

Key categories of loans include conventional conforming loans, FHA loans, VA loans, USDA loans, jumbo loans, and bank statement loans, which are only for self-employed borrowers. This last loan is only for the self-employed because of TRID, which stands for TILA-RESPA Integrated Disclosures.

TRID applies to most mortgage transactions secured by real estate and refers to new guidelines set by the Frank Dodd Act after the mortgage market meltdown. One very critical requirement baked into TRID is to adequately judge the borrower's ability to repay, or ATR. Lenders now have a critical burden of proof over the life of the loan. If a borrower goes through foreclosure and challenges the bank, then the burden of proof falls on the lender to establish that they appropriately assessed the borrower's ability to repay. They must prove they carefully documented the borrower's income and justifiably found the person was in a position from the start to make the payments.

How Have Banks Responded to These Regulations?

They've absolutely had to comply and we've seen lower default ratings. The mortgage market is much healthier. People have documented their ability to repay the loan and lenders are offering loans with more caution. The lender knows if they don't follow the rules and there's a lawsuit in the future, they will be required to give back the principle balance of the loan and all interest payments collected. The regulations force the bank to make sure they're following these rules every single time or they'll be on the hook for the money.

Bank statement loans for self-employed borrowers basically allow people to document their income using bank statements rather than tax returns. The interest rates for these loans are higher, but often people who are self-employed don't have two years of tax returns needed for a conventional conforming loan; they're selling businesses, they're buying businesses, or they're moving money from point A to point B—there's no way for a Fannie Mae-conforming underwriter to match that person's financials up with a conforming loan.

Who Else Might Want A Loan Like This?

High net-worth individuals who have lots of movement in their tax returns could also benefit from this type of loan. For example, a client may have sold their business last year and netted 800,000. If they printed out a profit, loss, and balance sheet, their tax returns would indicate they only made 30,000 a year because they're starting fresh in a different market. In this case, they wouldn't qualify for a conventional loan but would qualify for a bank statement loan based on the criteria.

The movie *The Big Short* provides great examples of these types of loans: bank statement loans for self-employed people aren't packaged up and sold on a secondary mortgage market. They're serviced by the people that make the loans, so the rules are a little different. They document the income based on their risk tolerance for those types of loans. Typically, they're made to people with higher net worth who have the money, the good credit, and the ability to repay the loans, but their tax returns don't look like a standard conforming borrower's tax returns.

What Are the Loan Parameters?

For guidance on parameters limits, ballpark interest rates, and amortization, consider that loan limits are up to five million with 30-year amortization. Fixed rate and adjustable rate terms apply in extremely broad measures. For context, think of terms like a 20% down payment with a 660 credit score.

Can a Borrower Buy A Commercial Property?

Commercial property is a different ball game and a much more competitive one. The TRID and the ability-to-repay rules don't apply.

How Much More in Interest than for a Conforming Loan?

General ballpark numbers sit as one to two percent higher, depending on the loan-to-value and the borrower's credit score for the overall risk variances associated with the borrower.

What's the Lowest Down Payment for this Loan?

For perspective, the lowest down payment we offer is 10%.

What Price Level Do Borrowers Typically Target?

We typically see purchases of higher priced homes. In Arizona, the maximum conforming loan amount is $510,400. Usually, we see people purchasing with loan amounts above that dollar amount, between a $500,000 loan amount and up to five million.

Chapter 2

When Do Jumbo Loans Come In To Play?

It's important to understand how each loan is useful for different circumstances. The jumbo loan can be up to 2 million, but if the borrower finances over 780,000, they need a 20% down payment. The interest rates are closer to conforming loan interest rates. In fact, the jumbo loan starts at $1 above conforming loan amounts. As an example, for Arizona as of May 28th, 2020, a loan amount of 510,401 would be considered jumbo.

At What Point are Jumbo Loans Common?

Jumbo loans usually start at 650 and go up from there. To avoid the need to take out a jumbo loan, borrowers can meet the down payment and conforming loan requirement by taking out a second mortgage or a second line of credit behind a conforming amount. For jumbo amounts, the operating range is from 600 to two million. Borrowers can get away with a 10% down payment in Arizona if they finance for less than 780,000. Otherwise, they're at a 20% down payment requirement. For jumbo loans, amortization is usually 30 years with an interest rate of about a half to 1% higher than a conforming loan. Sometimes lenders try to match their jumbo loans to the conforming loan limit to generate business, so borrowers should check frequently if they're considering a jumbo loan to see what rates are.

What Are the Requirements for Credit Score and Down Payment?

The credit score should be at 740, but a lot of times when I work with clients who have a 720 score who want this loan, they're borrowing with self-employed bank statement loans. There's a lot we can do to improve their credit and help them get from 720 to 740 if they have available cash. For example, we can use their money to pay down debt or take other similar measures to help them quickly boost their credit score into better loan territory. Jumbo loans are still offered by a few banks and a few lenders, but it's important to call for details. We just don't know their current parameters.

CHAPTER 3

WHAT ARE CONVENTIONAL OR CONFORMING LOANS?

This chapter covers Fannie Mae and Freddie Mac conforming or conventional loans, which are considered the sweet spot of mortgage lending. These borrowers have good to excellent credit scores, usually at 680, and put from 3% to 20% down (or more). These loans have a minimum credit score of 620 and require no negative credit history in the last 24 months. However, if a borrower comes into these loans with that minimum 620 credit score, they really should put 20% down. If they are not able to, an FHA (Federal Housing Administration) loan would be a better fit.

What Are Fannie Mae and Freddie Mac?

Freddie Mac refers to the Federal Home Loan Mortgage Corporation (FHLMC). Currently, it's under government conservatorship. Freddie Mac buys mortgages on the secondary market, pools them, and then sells them as mortgage-backed securities to investors. Fannie Mae does essentially the same thing, but buys from larger banks.

Fannie Mae's official name is the Federal National Mortgage Association (FNMA). It's also a government-sponsored enterprise (GSE). They secure mortgage loans in the form of mortgage-backed securities, allowing lenders to reinvest their assets in more lending; this effectively increases the number of lenders in the mortgage market.

Here's an example of how this mightwork: Fannie Mae may take a thousand $100,000 loans and turn them into a 1 million or $100 million security. Then, they'll take that $100 million security to the Oklahoma state pension retirement fund and say, "Hey, give us 100 million dollars. You can own the security and each month as people make their mortgage payments, your investment grows over time." Fannie Mae then takes that $100 million and buys another $100 million for somebody else, and then sells that to the country of Iceland.

The government agrees to make this liquid type of lending widely available with very clear variables. The risk of people buying the securities is well understood—there are rigid rules, such as brokers having to follow the ability to repay the loan or suffer the consequences.

What Are Typical Down Payments?

While it's possible to put a minimum of 3% down on conventional and conforming loans, the typical amount is 5% down, which requires a higher interest rate and higher mortgage insurance. The sweet spot for a conforming loan is a 740-credit score with around 10% down and a great work history and no negative credit in the past two years.

What Are the Other Negative Consequences of that 3% Down?

The loan level pricing adjustments that affect conventional loans are more expensive with lower credit scores and lower down payments. Therefore, to fully take advantage of a conventional loan offering, borrowers should consider putting 10% down and have a credit score of at least 680. Otherwise, an FHA loan works almost as well. The higher the credit score and down payment, the more attractive a conforming loan or loan amount is.

What Are Current Loan Limits in Arizona?

Loan limits are county-specific in Arizona, but they tend to be around the same figure: $510,400, which is the conforming loan limit for Maricopa County. On the other hand, counties in California vary with some high-cost counties.

Chapter 4

When Is Mortgage Insurance Required?

Fannie Mae and Freddie Mac will only insure loans with up to an 80% loan-to-value. They will, however, purchase loans between 80.01% and 97.00% if the loans have mortgage insurance or private mortgage insurance. Basically, the homeowner has to pay to insure the amount borrowed over 80% of the purchase price of the home. While the mortgage insurance premium only protects the investor, the homeowner benefits because they don't have to make a 20% down payment. The downside remains that the homeowner has to pay for this insurance policy every month in addition to their mortgage payment.

How Can a Homeowner Predict the Mortgage Insurance Amount?

If the below still leaves questions, please contact me for details, but here's some basic information:

The technological revolution changed this process through the spread of information. Before access to computing power, typically there'd be 15, 20, and 30-year terms for conforming loan amounts; however, the banks gained a better sense of homeowner needs and now cater towards everyone's individual mortgage demands. Banks have realized that people don't want to necessarily start their loan over every time they refinance.

Now, depending on whom a homeowner works with, they might find a lender who will cater to their specific timeframe. Let's say for example, they took out a 30-year loan six years ago and today want to refinance to a lower rate, but don't want to start a new 30-year loan. They'd rather start a 24-year loan to keep on track with their current payment schedule. That's easily found in today's mortgage market, and they can expect to see 18, 19, 20, 21, and 22-year terms—even 22 and three-month terms. Basically, a homeowner can expect to get whatever type of loan term they want. They might may pay a slight premium for that, but not necessarily.

CHAPTER 5

WHAT ARE FHA LOANS FOR?

An FHA loan is designed for low to moderate income borrowers who want to make as little a down payment as the minimum of 3.5%, which can be gifted. While a borrower might find their conventional loan only requires a 3% down payment, the FHA generally allows credit scores as low as 580. (During this time of COVID, that score has been increased to 620, but we expect it to go back to 580 post-COVID.)

Essentially, it's easier to qualify for a loan under FHA. While 3.5% is the minimum down payment, because FHA allows a much lower credit score, the credit and work history can be spotty. Conventional loans might require letters of explanation for negative items on the credit report or substandard work history. An FHA loan has easier parameters and it's not as tough to be eligible.

However, because it's easier to qualify, there's a higher risk of default for the general FHA pool of loans; therefore, the mortgage insurance premium is more expensive. As of May 28, 2020, borrowers can expect to pay a 1.75% fee that's added to the loan as an upfront cost and goes directly to the FHA. Borrowers can also expect to pay a monthly factor of 0.85%. For example, on a $200,000 loan, they would pay $141.67 a month; therefore, the mortgage insurance premium is higher than what's expected for a conventional loan. So, while borrowers with more negative credit blemishes can get a loan, they're paying a higher mortgage insurance premium for that benefit.

How Would a Good Mortgage Broker Handle This?

An experienced and savvy mortgage broker will know how to balance these issues and how to appropriately explain the process to a borrower. For some circumstances, for example, instead of approaching them with, "Yeah, you have to take an FHA loan," a broker could say, "Listen, I've identified some items on your credit report. If we get it taken care of and if you can maybe save X amount over the next four months, it's better to hold off and, assuming things stay the same four months from now, you'll save $250 a month. Let's work on your application over that period, rather than jumping into something that's less economically savory for you and your family." It's important to offer this bigger picture and various scenarios to give borrowers helpful goals as well as understand alternative conditions like the following.

What's a First-Time Home Buyer and Is It an Advantage?

A buyer can have owned a house before and be considered a first-time home buyer if they're going to use a down payment assistance program. These basically are down payment grants that come in the form of repayable or forgivable grants. However, some of those grants require no home ownership over the last 36 months. Grants are different than the FHA and conventional loan programs.

As a first-time home buyer, both FHA and conventional loans are available based on the buyer's financial situation, credit history, and work history. If they can meet the conventional loan requirements, they're much better off going with a conventional loan from the beginning because their mortgage insurance premium will be less, even if they put the same 3.5% or 5% down. If they're a first-time home buyer and can put 10% down, have been on the same job for two years, and have great credit, they don't want to use an FHA loan because they'll pay less of a mortgage insurance premium.

However, it's important to consider different buyer situations. For example, there might be a first-time home buyer who's also a first-time mother. Furthermore, this buyer has been out of work for six months last year and is just returning to work. An FHA loan would be the only way that this buyer could get financing.

In a nutshell, an FHA indicates more relaxed lending qualifications and guidelines with a higher mortgage insurance premium cost. It's up to the mortgage broker to help buyers known when that cost is worth it and when it's better to wait.

CHAPTER 6

WHAT'S A USDA LOAN?

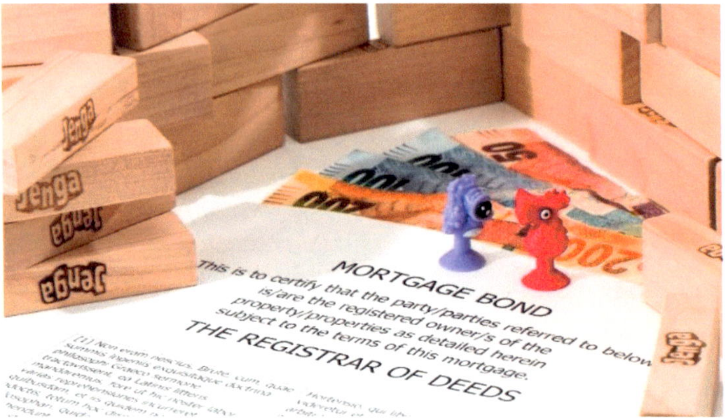

The United States Department of Agriculture, or USDA, offers a rural development home loan. A USDA home loan is basically a zero-down home loan meant for low to moderate income home buyers who purchase a home within very rigid geographical areas outlined by the USDA.

How Are Rural Areas Designated?

Understanding how "rural areas" are defined can be confusing. Does an area have to be in the middle of nowhere to fit the bill? While there are exceptions usually associated with suburban sprawl, the basic answer is yes, they do. If someone wants to buy in a sparsely-populated area, they can get a USDA loan.

Rural area designations are based on population density. Obviously, though, density can change rather quickly. Let's look at, for example, the Phoenix Metro area. Ten years ago, a buyer could have taken out a rural loan in the Southeast Valley, anywhere southeast of Gilbert Road and Queen Creek road. Currently, because the population has grown in the Southeast Valley and there's a much higher population density southeast of Gilbert and Queen Creek based on census records, that boundary no longer works as a qualifying line. Very few parts of Queen Creek are now eligible, and neither are some parts of San Tan Valley. Therefore, while some areas close to a Metro area might qualify, most probably won't or may not within a span of a few years.

Readers interested in buying in the USDA territory can call me and I'll send a link for the maps. While there are very rigid geographic boundaries, we can review the maps together and I can explain the logistics.

There are also very rigid income limitations. As with some previous loan types, this is for a low to moderate income household. If a buyer makes more than a certain income, they will not qualify. The income amount is assessed according to where they live as well as other factors. For an example, consider someone living in Maricopa County. Based on the area's median income and the number of people in the household, the USDA establishes maximum income limits for loan qualification purposes. Generally, though, a buyer only needs to worry about minimum income limits. However, the debt-to-income ratio can't be higher than 42%.

Here's an example with more specific numbers: in Maricopa County, imagine a household with eight people. The guaranteed rural housing loan program allows this household to make up to $119,200 and still qualify. Because there's no down payment required and the mortgage insurance premium is much lower than for FHA, it helps to compare a USDA with a conventional loan when buying in a rural area. In most cases, a USDA loan is the best option because the buyer doesn't have to make any down payment.

Another great aspect is associated with the appraised versus purchase price. Generally, on a conventional or FHA loan, if the appraised value comes in higher than the purchase price, it's a nice bonus but there's no immediate benefit. The borrower has to use the lower of the two for the loan terms to establish the maximum loan ceiling. However, with a USDA loan, if the value comes in higher than the purchase price, the borrower can use that money to pay for closing costs and/or make repairs to the house.

So, if a seller sold a house for $150,000 and the appraisal comes in at $175,000, the buyer can elect to use that $25,000 to a) pay closing costs, b) make repairs to the house, or c) pay off debt to qualify. Again, a USDA loan doesn't act like a conventional loan in a number of ways. There are several motivating benefits for folks who are purchasing in rural areas to use that money to buy as well as for first-time home buyers who just don't have the down payment available.

CHAPTER 7

WHAT'S A VA LOAN AND WHO QUALIFIES?

The VA loan is my favorite loan and has a great origin story. It all started with soldiers fighting alongside George Washington in the revolutionary war. When the war was over, these same soldiers were given land in America based on their rank. After the American revolution, they were able to leave the military and take possession of this land and use it how they wished, most commonly to farm.

The VA loan is a continuation of that American tradition. Military members with some basic services requirements (discussed below) are given the VA home loan eligibility as a benefit. What benefit does it offer? Earlier I explained how Fannie Mae and Freddie Mac require everybody who doesn't make a 20% down payment on their house to take out mortgage insurance. Basically, the VA loan provides free mortgage insurance. A veteran can borrow a hundred percent of the value of their home without paying monthly mortgage insurance. While there is a one-time VA funding fee that's added to the loan, I've never seen it being paid out of pocket. Rather, it's always added to the loan. That VA funding fee helps pay back lenders for insurance losses from veterans who have gone into foreclosure. Veterans pay a one-time fee of as little as a .5% or as high as 3.6%. As of March 28th, 2020, that VA funding fee pool insures all the lenders who are making 100% loans to veterans. Another great caveat: any veteran who has a 10% or more VA service-related disability does not have to pay that funding fee.

The basic service requirements include the following: at least 24 months consecutive active duty or at least six years in the guard or national reserves with at least one weekend a month. In other words, the military member must have served six years of weekend duty or two years active duty or a combination thereof. Feel free to call me with questions about this. A lot of veterans don't know how to go about checking their eligibility. They might have lost their DD 214, or don't know how to go about finding it. If a veteran is eligible for their VA home loan, it will be indicated on a document called a certificate of eligibility and I can help with that.

Before the Department of Defense went from analog to digital, from filing cabinets to online cloud storage, a lot of veterans didn't know where to go. They would have gone to their place of duty where they enlisted or contacted an old location that had been shut down; therefore, it was hard to find the documents. But digital and cloud storage have helped free up this information. Again, if a veteran doesn't know where to go, they can contact me and we can start the search to find out more. Basically, the information has all been consolidated into one place. I can help fill in missing details with research and get to the bottom of finding their eligibility records. It may take up to a month or two in a worst-case scenario, but it's definitely attainable.

The VA loan is set up in a way that is very non-restrictive. Keep in mind that conventional loans have the most restrictive guidelines while FHA loans are the least restrictive thus far. However, VA loan guidelines are even less restrictive than FHA guidelines. The VA offers the lowest interest rates of all VA, FHA, and conventional combined. Generally speaking, the VA rates is a half percent lower than a conventional rate in addition to these least restrictive guidelines. These guidelines include lower credit scores, less stringent work history requirements, and higher debt-to-income ratios. With a conventional loan, a borrower may not get an automated approval through Fannie Mae and Freddie Mac's automated underwriting software with more than a 45% debt-to-income ratio. In many cases, I've seen automated approvals through the VA's automated underwriting interface of 70% debt-to-income ratio or higher, with no need to document the veteran's income.

The Department of Veterans Affairs wants every veteran to exercise their benefit of home ownership. The government wants veterans to own homes. There are many reasons, including looking bad if veterans are on the street. Because they want veterans to own homes, the guidelines are loose and the rates are low.

What Are Some of The Requirements?

In alignment with these looser requirements, there's no down payment required on a purchase up to a million. Buying a million-dollar home in Arizona and don't have a down payment? No problem, for a veteran. Does the borrower has some side money-making gig that can't be documented on a conventional loan? No problem. There's a higher debt-to-income ratio allowed on a VA loan. Credit problems? A foreclosure or a bankruptcy that would make a borrower ineligible for a conventional loan based on their conventional loan matrix? Waiting time periods? All these are more than likely no problem under a VA loan. In fact, there's less time required from a major derogatory credit event to getting a VA loan than with a conventional loan.

What Happens under an Other Than Honorable Or Dishonorable Discharge?

Generally speaking, a dishonorable discharge means the former service member won't have a certificate of eligibility. However, an other than honorable discharge, depending on the nature of the discharge and time served, may not preclude access to the VA home loan benefit.

Call for details.

CHAPTER 8

WHAT ARE THE CONSEQUENCES OF REFINANCING?

For a self-employed bank statement loan the borrower can refinance, but they really aren't going to benefit unless, a) they took out an adjustable rate mortgage and are at the end of their adjustable rate mortgage time period, or b) they're in a phase of their career where they no longer need to qualify bank statements and are eligible to qualify with full tax returns.

Are the Requirements as Stringent as a First Loan?

A borrower may have a prepayment penalty associated with the bank statement loan, or may not because it's not a TRID loan or a Fannie Mae/ Freddie Mac insured loan. The lenders have unique requirements that are sometimes harsher than a conventional or other government-backed loan. Really, what prevented the borrower from getting a conventional loan at a lower rate is what led them to a bank statement loan for self-employed people to begin with, so unless they qualify with bank statements or their rate has adjusted and their monthly payment has gone up, they probably are in the best loan for their circumstances. Essentially, if they've done a self-employed loan and are not at the point of refinancing into a conforming loan, then it's probably not going to help.

Do People with Existing Jumbos Tend To Refinance and Is It Beneficial?

When the loan limits have increased or jumbo rates have gone down, it might make sense to consider a new Jumbo loan with a lower interest rate. Because market conditions have improved, it may seem a logical step. Alternatively, a borrower might be in position to take one Jumbo loan and turn it into two loans. The first of the two would be a conventional conforming loan, which is lower than the county loan limit, with a second mortgage behind it. This results in a much lower interest rate and payment.

What Are Other Reasons To Jumboize?

There are several reasons. For example, an owner may need to borrow money from their home's equity, and want to increase their jumbo loan amount from 800,000 to 1.4 million. That's called a "cash out" jumbo loan. This is a rate and term refinance: the owner would take the same amount that's owed from a higher interest rate because market conditions improved. They would finance that same amount with a much lower interest rate through this rate and term refinance. Rate and term indicates that those are the only things changing while there's no cash out. The owner is not saying, "Hey, I need 20 grand to go to Vegas or take that vacation or buy that car." Either they no longer need a jumbo loan or they need to take cash out to finance something else and can't find a cheaper rate than their home mortgage for that need.

Is There a Reason to Do A Term Refinance Versus A Rate?

It's either a rate and term or cash out. The owner can refinance again at a lower rate, which is going to give them a lower payment, but it's also going to start the term over again.

What Are Benefits of Refinancing a Conventional Conforming?

Benefits of refinancing a conventional conforming loan include paying off the house sooner and improving cash flow. That means we finance the rate of X to X minus half a percent or X minus 1%, depending on the external market conditions. An owner may want to refinance their conventional loan for debt consolidation to payoff higher interest rate credit cards. Or, they may want to take cash out to pay for their kids' education—there are several reasons that make sense. Whatever the need, if the owner can't find a cheaper way to finance their lifestyle needs, a lot of times their home equity loans and rates they'll get on their mortgage are going to be lower than what they're going to get elsewhere. Plus, because it's on a 30-year amortization schedule, they're more than likely going to have the lowest payment available as well by taking cash out of their home.

What Kinds of Loans Can You Refinance Into?

It depends on the need. Owners can refinance from a conventional to an FHA, from a VA to a conventional, and from a USDA to a conventional. It just depends on what they are looking to do and their qualifications at the time of the refinance request. Based on what they are attempting to do, what their needs are, or what their goals are, we would work with them to find out which loan is best at that time of refinance.

Once they have 22% or more of equity in their house, does the mortgage insurance just fall off or do they have to refinance to get rid of it on a conventional?

The benefit of conventional mortgage insurance is that when there's a 22% equity or more in a house, the mortgage insurance as of March 28th, 2020, will come off. There are two ways to make this happen. First, an owner can call a lender and ask them to order an appraisal because they think the current market value of their home indicates a 20% equity in their home. They would then pay for the appraisal. If they're right, the mortgage insurance would come off. If they're wrong, the mortgage insurance stays and their loss is the money spent on an appraisal. Second, the owner can pay down their mortgage balance to 78% of the original purchase price or the amount financed on their current loan.

With both FHA and VA loan, there's a streamlined refinance process. Normal refinancing protocol is to document income, assets, and the appraised value of the home. Those are all the documents required for a regular refinance, whether it's a rate term or cash out. However, with FHA and VA loans, the amount of documentation required is considerably less. No appraisals are required, no verification of income is required, and if there's no cash to close, then no assets are required to be documented either. It's a much simpler process that involves a verbal verification or a written verification of employment from the borrower's employer at time of refinance stating that they're currently employed. In addition to being an easier process, it's also much more affordable: the borrower doesn't have to pay for the appraisal, so the fees are lower on an FHA loan. All in all, it's quicker and easier.

Because when they've been making their payments on time the rates drop, it allows people with FHA and VA loans to enable this rate drop without going through the arduous process of documenting everything again. It's a quick and easy way to save money on their mortgage through a streamlined refinance.

Before considering discussing a refinance with a loan or mortgage professional, homeowners really need to have in mind a timeframe for how long they plan on making payments on their mortgage. They should not call a seasoned, trained salesperson about refinancing until they know how long they are planning on making payments on their home. Otherwise, homeowners may be sold something that they do not want or need and could lose thousands of dollars. Mortgage bankers or brokers are in the business to sell mortgages and because they're trained sales professionals, they may easily convince a client to refinance without having considered their long-term goals and objectives. While this likely won't benefit a client, it usually benefits the broker. It's best to do the research and make a plan before that call. Hopefully, this book helped along the way.

INDEX

B

bankruptcy · 37

C

Cash Out Jumbo Loan · 41

COVID · 26

D

Dishonorable Discharge · 38

F

Fannie Mae · 20

FHA loan · 26

FNMA · 20

foreclosure · 37

Freddie Mac · 20

M

mortgage insurance premium · 29

O

Other Than Honorable Discharge · 38

R

refinance · 39

repayable grants · 28

T

tax returns · 39

U

USDA · 30

V

VA loan · 35

Notes

Made in the USA
Monee, IL
05 November 2026

67385066R00031